E
MO

Moncure, Jane Belk

Short "a" and long
"a" play a game

DATE			
OC 30 '85	NO 12 '88	JUL 14 '94	AG 07 '0
NO 13 '85	JY 20 '89	SEP 22 '94	JY 14 '03
NO 29 '85	SE 22 '89	FEB 08 '95	NO 28 '0
MY 17 '86	JA 29 '90	JUL 28 '95	
JE 06 '86	FE 20 '90	JUN 06 '96	
JE 21 '86	JY 26 '90	JUL 30 '96	
	DE 20 '90	SEP 03 '96	NO 2
JY 7 '86	AG 12 '91	JAN 22 '97	A 2 8 '0
AP 15 '87	JY 8 '92	FEB 11 '97	
AG 14 '87	MR 15 '93	OCT 08 '9	
SE 11 '87	SE 15 '93	NO 10 '99	
	OC 1 '93	MY 15 00	

© THE BAKER & TAYLOR CO.

Short a and Long a
Play
a Game

written by Jane Belk Moncure
illustrated by Helen Endres

THE CHILD'S WORLD

ELGIN, ILLINOIS 60120

Library of Congress Cataloging in Publication Data

Moncure, Jane Belk.
  Short ''a'' and Long ''a'' play a game.

  (Play with vowel sounds)
  SUMMARY: Introduces the long and short ''a'' sounds.
  1. English language—Vowels—Juvenile literature.
[1. English language—Vowels] I. Endres, Helen.
II. Title. III. Series.
PE1157.M6   428'.1   79-10300
ISBN 0-89565-089-4

Distributed by Childrens Press, 1224 West Van Buren Street,
Chicago, Illinois 60607.

Short a and Long a

Play
a Game

This is . He has a special sound.

Alligator
begins with his short "a" sound.

So does apple.

apple

alligator

This is  . She has a different sound.

Ape begins with
her long "a" sound.

8

So does apron.

ape

apron

Can you hear the short a and the long a sounds?

apple

alligator

One day,  said, "Let's play a game. I will look for my sound in words.

ape

apron

long a

And you can look for your sound in words. We'll see who can find the most words."

found an arrow,

an ax,

an ant,

and an astronaut.

"I will win!" he said.

found acorns

and an angel.

"No! I will win!" she said.

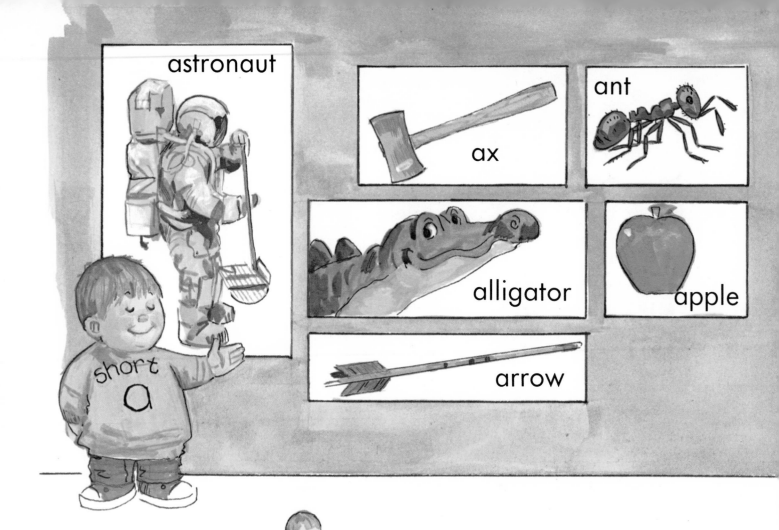

astronaut

ax

ant

alligator

apple

arrow

counted. "I win," he said. "I have the most words."

apron

acorns

ape

angel

 counted. "No! No! No!" she said.

''I will use my eyes

and ears.

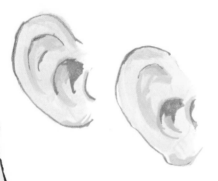

My sound hides in words.
I will find words with my sound
in the middle of them.''

18

found a rake,

a cake,

a lake,

and a snake.

Then  found a cape

for the ape,

and grapes  for the ape.

"Now I win!" said .

"No! No! No!" said  .

"I will use my eyes and my ears.
My sound hides in words too. I will find
words with my sound in the middle of
them."

short a found a camel,

a cat

with a bat,

and a rat.

Then a found rabbits

and radishes

for the rabbits.

"Now I win!" said

25

cat

ant

apple

camel

astronaut

rat

radishes

ax

alligator

rabbits

arrow

bat

short a

Can you tel

lake

cake

cape

grapes

apron

rake

angel

ape

snake

acorns

long a

who won?

Can you read more words with  short a ?

flag

crab

parrot

fan

pan

hat

acrobat

tadpole

can

mat

Can you read more words with long a ?

gate

whale

cage

radio

paint

skates

cane

plate

train

Now, you make up a game!